MW01267555

WHITE BUFFALO WOMAN

AN INDIAN LEGEND

By Christine Crowl

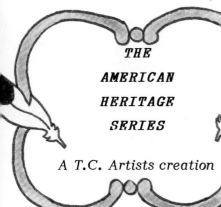

*THE
AMERICAN
HERITAGE
SERIES*

A T.C. Artists creation

Lovingly dedicated to our Native American youth.

ISBN 1-877976-10-5

LONG AGO, there lived a mighty nation of people. Their numbers were so great that they divided into seven tribes. They spread themselves far across the plains of North America. Together, this great nation was called "The Seven Council Fires" of the Sioux.

Many summers past, all seven tribes had come together to sit at one camp. The sun rose each day and the green grass grew tall beneath its warmth. Songbirds greeted the people each morning and the breeze smelled sweet with the perfume of fresh flowers.

This should have been a happy time for the Sioux. Instead, the people were very sad. No animals had come to the prairie that summer, and the people were hungry. Everyday they sent their young men out to search for game. Each night the hunters came back without any meat for their families.

"The four-leggeds have left us to starve!" the people cried. "Is there no one who can bring them back?"

Standing Hollow Horn was chief of the *Without Bows* tribe. He heard the little children crying in his camp. Their tears made him sad. He wondered what he could do to end their hunger. The mystery puzzled him. He thought his people had done something to anger the animal spirits.

The next day, he sent two of his own hunters in search of meat.

Strong Bow was a handsome brave of twenty. He was the best hunter in his tribe. His aim was always careful and his arrows never missed. Of all the hunters, Strong Bow owned the most hides. The chief knew if there was game to be found, Strong Bow would not miss.

Eagle Eyes was only fourteen winters old, but he was the best scout of all. Because of his keen eyesight, he could find small tracks where most scouts saw none. Even the footprints of a tiny mouse never eluded his eyes. The chief knew if there was game to be found, Eagle Eyes would find it.

It was a time before the Sioux owned horses, so the two braves set out on foot. They searched far and wide. After many hours they still could find no animals. Even the green prairie, where the buffalo grazed, was quiet and still.

"Perhaps if we climb that hill we could get a better look," Eagle Eyes said. "Surely, there must be something hiding in the tall grass. Even a rabbit would be better than nothing."

Strong Bow followed the young scout up the hillside. When they reached the top, Eagle Eyes saw something moving.

"Can you tell what it is?" Strong Bow asked. But the sun was too bright. The boy could only make out a tiny speck. As it came closer, they saw that it moved very strangely. The figure seemed to be floating on air.

"It's a woman!" Eagle Eyes exclaimed. "A sacred woman!"

Strong Bow squinted his eyes to make out the form. As she came near, both young braves stood gazing open-mouthed.

The woman was more beautiful than any they had seen. She wore a gleaming, white dress. Her long, black hair reflected the very rays of the sun. It almost hurt their eyes to look at her. There were two red circles painted on her cheeks and she carried a strange bundle wrapped in buffalo hide.

Strong Bow was enchanted. He reached out to touch the sacred woman.

Suddenly there was a great rumbling in the sky. A bolt of lightning flew down from the clouds and struck the bold hunter. In a puff of smoke, Strong Bow was gone!

Eagle Eyes trembled with fear. He knew his friend had been punished. He had shown disrespect towards the sacred woman. The young scout was afraid something worse might happen to him.

"Do not be frightened, Young Man," the woman said. "I have come to bring you a message. Her voice sounded like a song. Eagle Eyes was no longer afraid.

"What will you have me do?" he asked.

"Go back to your people and tell them I am coming. Ask your chief to build a big Medicine-Lodge. Tell him to use twenty-four poles. In the center of this lodge he must put red earth on the floor. On top of this, place a buffalo skull and a three-stick rack. This sacred altar will hold the gift I am bringing to your people."

Eagle Eyes ran all the way home. "Someone sacred is coming!" he cried, racing through the camp. "A holy woman is coming. Everyone make ready for her!"

The Crier went to each lodge and spread the news. The people joined together and raised a giant tipi. They used twenty-four of the tallest pine trees they could find. In the center they made a sacred altar, just as the woman had asked. When finished, the people waited: first one day... then two...then three...

Finally, on the fourth day, they saw a strange form appear over the horizon. The gleaming, white dress glowed from afar. Standing Hollow Horn was the first to greet the sacred woman. He invited her inside the new Medicine-Lodge. The people followed.

The young woman entered the tipi. She walked around, circling sunwise. She then knelt before the altar and traced a design in the red dirt with her finger. Again, she stood up and circled the lodge four more times.

"My movements are like the sun," she said. "I am walking the road of life, a circle without end."

Carefully she untied her bundle and showed the people her gift. It was the very first pipe the Sioux had ever seen. She held it up for everyone to see.

The woman began to sing a song. Then she filled the pipe with red willow-bark. Lighting it, she said, "This is a fire without end. This flame will be handed down from generation to generation. The smoke that rises up is the breath of the Great Spirit."

She then taught the people how to pray with the pipe. She showed them how to lift it towards the sky, down towards the earth, then to each of the four directions.

"With this pipe," she said, "the people will walk like a prayer. When your feet are touching the earth and the pipe is reaching towards the sky, your body forms a bridge between heaven and earth. The pipe will join you together with all living things. You will be one with the earth, the sky, the trees, and the animals. The Great Spirit is our father. All that he has created are related as brothers. You are one big family. You must take care of each other. The earth and animals will feed and clothe you. In return, you must take good care of them. The pipe will keep you together until the end of time.

The sacred woman then spoke to the women. She told them that they were just as important as the men.

"You are the mothers of future nations," she said. "You do all the hard work and keep the people alive. What you do is just as great as what the warriors do. That is why the pipe is something the men and women share together. The men will make the pipe, but the women will decorate it. When a man and a woman are joined in marriage, they will hold the pipe at the same time. Their hands will be wrapped together, thus binding them for life."

The woman then taught her sisters many new things. Afterwards, she spoke to their children. "You are the most important people of all," she told them. "You will be the future men and women of this tribe. Someday you will also hold the pipe. When you have children of your own, you must teach them how to pray with it. In this way the pipe will be handed down from generation to generation."

The sacred woman called all the people together for one last time. "Remember," she said, "the pipe is very sacred. Treat it with respect and it will take care of you."

The people watched as the woman walked away towards the setting sun. As they were admiring her, she suddenly stopped and rolled on the ground four times. The first time she turned into a black buffalo. The second time she turned into a brown one. On the third turn she changed into a red one. On the fourth turn, a white buffalo rose up to stand against the setting sun. A white buffalo, the most holy thing a man could ever see. By doing this, the sacred woman knew that the people would not marvel at her beauty. Instead, they would remember the important message she had brought them.

The sacred, white buffalo then dissappeared. Not long after, the buffalo herds came back to the plains. The people were no longer hungry. They lived happily for many years. Always they would remember the laws brought by White Buffalo Woman.